STRUGGLE HAS ITS STRENGTHS

Aquanda Stanfield Cummings

STRUGGLE HAS ITS STRENGTHS

A WOMAN'S GUIDE TO WINNING WHILE HEALING EMOTIONAL WOUNDS

Aquanda Stanfield Cummings

Aquanda Stanfield Cummings

Struggle Has Its Strengths

Copyright © 2015 by Aquanda Stanfield Cummings

ISBN 978-0-9961069-0-0

DEDICATION

This book is dedicated to the woman that doesn't want to give up, but doesn't know how to move forward.

Dear God,

Thank you for teaching me how to love "life" when I felt as though "life" did not love me. Thank you for giving me the humility to be honest about what pain took from me and the courage to take it back. Although, I thought my circumstances served me a death sentence; your guidance, grace, and mercy has given me double for my trouble and the understanding that we grow when it "rains." God bless this conversation and the woman I am having it with. Let your inspiration and my life lessons serve as a pep talk when she needs one and may my journey breathe life into hers. Amen

ACKNOWLEDGMENTS

To my husband Kendrick thank you for always supporting my efforts and loving me flaws and all. I love you.

To my son Kendrick II you have taught me patience and the true nature of God's love for your father and me.

To my mother, Joyce Stanfield thank you for teaching me how to worship God with my whole self and always supporting my dreams.

To my father, William Stanfield Jr. thank you for holding me to high standards and giving me a strong work ethic by watching your example.

To my brothers and sisters thank you for your brutal honesty and always being there for me.

To my grandparents, William and Mable Stanfield thank you for always having my back and always providing our family with a "happy place."

To my Grandmother Sally and Grandfather Clarence I wish you were here.

To the rest of my family and friends thank you for your support and I love each of you.

CONTENTS

INTRODUCTION

As women, many of us get so caught up in our own struggles that we fail to realize that we are the life support system for everything and everybody around us. We are not only the givers of life, but the mental and emotional preservers of it, as well. Clichés like, "happy wife, happy life" and "if momma isn't happy nobody's happy" are absolutely true. The well-being of every person under the sound of your voice is hanging in the balance when you allow your brokenness to become your bondage.

As an educator, I've watched children walk into classrooms mentally and emotionally damaged by the dysfunction in their homes and teachers are forced to sacrifice instructional time to build self-esteem and handle the disciplinary issues of those that used the classroom as a place to vent their frustrations. The classroom should represent new beginnings and opportunities for children and their families; however, there are negative forces in many of our households that make this opportunity almost impossible to take advantage of. These forces have taken our homes from safe havens to breeding grounds for struggle, and before many of these children get to choose their own path they are already damaged goods by no fault of their own. They walk into classrooms suffering from abuse, depression, anxiety, anger, and all of the other by-products of a dysfunctional home environment. The home environment by definition is the condition in which a person lives. The most common causes of dysfunction in the home environment are associated with:

•Who you allow in your home;

•The activities that take place in the dwelling;

•The negativity you ignore; and

•The absence of appropriate standards.

Arguably, the main cause of household dysfunction involves the bad habits and lifestyle choices of the adults in the home. These children are suffering from the effects of your emotional baggage, bad habits, insecurities, etc. I know many of you are thinking, "This does not apply to my household because we have our problems, but my children are fine." Are you sure? Anyone that lives in a dysfunctional environment for a prolonged period of time is at extremely high risk for damage to their mental-emotional health.

Mental-emotional health is characterized by:

- "How you feel about yourself;

- Your ability to manage your feelings;

- The quality of your relationships; and

- How you deal with difficulties."

Do you see how easily we can lose our children if their injuries are hiding in these places? This brings me to my next question: Does the environment in which you are raising your children provide positive examples of mental-emotional health? This is a tough question because it forces us, as parents, to look at who we are as people and the role our personal problems and preferences play in the lives of our children. When a child goes astray, parents at some point have to ponder their role in the child's behavior. Much of your answer lies in how well you managed your household environment and your own mental-emotional health. I once had a student who was very rude and disrespectful. She would physically attack students and teachers for the least thing. She was a very angry child. One day right before lunch she threatened me. I took the other students to the cafeteria and informed her that she would be eating with me in my classroom. As she and I approached the door my spirit said, "Don't punish her today, but ask her what's wrong. Try to see the world through her eyes." I took a deep breath and said, "I know what pain looks like and you are in pain. Would you like to talk about it?" She immediately started to cry. This fourteen year old, tough girl melted before my eyes. She began by telling me that she was being raised by her grandparents and although she loved them, she wanted to be with her mother. The student continued by saying that her mother had a nervous breakdown as a result of a bad relationship and currently lived in a mental institution. The little girl looked at me and said "She doesn't even know my name!" This child was so overcome with grief that she let out a long wale and almost fell out of her chair. I cried with her that day and also shared a few of my own struggles and how I overcame them. This child became a constant topic of conversation during my time with God. She never threatened me again. My experiences have taught me that the "apple never falls far from the tree" and where there are damaged children there are broken adults.

A woman that does not function with a reasonable portion of mental, physical, and emotional health becomes much more vulnerable to the negativity in the world and this unintentionally affects the well-being of her children, spouse, family, and friends.

I know how the blows of life can make you want to lay down your worth, your well-being, your body, and your virtue. However, if you could just muster up a "Not anymore" in your spirit and give God little room. He will show you how everything (even the ugly) you have gone through is necessary for his purpose in your life. You will eventually find the strength necessary to take your rightful place in your household and in your destiny.

Children serve as my greatest inspiration for writing this book; however, the content is dedicated to giving any woman who feels like "damaged goods" the understanding that wounded women win too.

1 BRUISES & BLESSINGS

"The LORD is close to the brokenhearted; he rescues those whose spirits are crushed."

Psalms 34:18

My motto in life has become "what happens might hurt me, but it won't hinder me!" Although, I have not always been this way. I have had my share of bumps and bruises and the scars to prove it, but I have also been blessed beyond what I ever thought possible. However, it wasn't until I got "sick and tired of being sick and tired" did I start building the bridge between the two (bruises and blessings). I was fed up with feeling "less than" and I was finally willing to admit that the first 25 years of my life were spent "crying over spilled milk." Many women, like myself, have led this miserable existence; wearing a mask of happiness and

9

contentment but secretly suffering.

Our emotional wounds have caused many of us to miss the fact that we are living the lives that we prayed for, living the lives of our dreams, or even more importantly, we have survived some very difficult days. However, we can't celebrate the mountains we've climbed because we are still obsessing over the emotional injuries we received along the way. Emotional injuries common to women stem from (but are not limited to):

- Loss of Loved Ones

- Childhood Issues

- Bad Relationships

- Abuses

- Neglect

• Physical Appearance

These are some very difficult injuries to overcome, but

they don't have to dictate the quality of your life.

Quality of life (or well-being) is the state of being

comfortable, healthy, happy, and productive. At this

very moment many of us can think about a past hurt

and get emotional (tears, anger, etc.). Why? The reason

is because you unconsciously carried that hurt in your

head and your heart from the time and place in which it

happened. You have dragged it around like a backpack

and contaminated every season of your life with it. As a

result you're chronically unhappy.

Take a second and think back over your life. How many

times has your emotional baggage cheated you out of a

"happily ever after?" I am not only referring to love

relationships, but some of us have abilities and skill sets that are not being utilized because we can't see passed our pain. There are others of us that have poured ourselves into our abilities, but lack the social and emotional skills to have healthy love relationships. I know the losses and setbacks that you have endured have left you with some deep-rooted wounds. But what you might not be aware of is that these wounds are negatively affecting the way you think, the decisions you make, and your ability to move forward.

Every area of struggle in your life is maintained by some source of pain. Some women have no "luck" in love because they have daddy issues. Others won't pursue any of their dreams because they believed those that said or treated them like they weren't good enough.

These sources can cripple even the strongest woman, but it's high time we turn the tables.

Forgive Yourself

You did it, you regret it, don't repeat it, and forget it!

First you have to forgive yourself. You can no longer allow what you have been through or what you have done to get in the way of winning. 1 John 1:9 states: "He is faithful and just to forgive us of our sins and to cleanse us from all unrighteousness." You prayed for forgiveness, but you never forgave yourself. God let it go when you asked him to and instead of operating on this promise you have allowed the pain you feel to paralyze your ability to be happy and productive. A woman that can't forgive herself can't win! She lives in guilt and doesn't feel that she is worthy of a better life. This explains why many of us treat blessing like a bad thing. Example, you prayed for financial stability and God blessed you with a good job, but you let a miserable coworker cause you to quit or get fired.

WORDS OF ~~WISDOM~~ WINNING

Satan <u>cannot</u> take what God gives you, but he will try to make you give it away. Blessing is never without testing.

Some women have secretly given up in many areas of their lives because they feel as though God has turned a deaf ear to them because of the sins they have committed or because of the consistency of their struggles. Ephesians 2: 4-5 states "…because of his great love for us, God, who is rich in mercy, made us alive with Christ even when we were dead in our transgressions….." I am a living witness that God will love you even when you are not sure how you feel about yourself. The reality is that the highest power in the universe is your father. So even when you are not sure *"who you are,"* be confident in *"whose you are."*

2 THE EVICTION

"You can't live here anymore!"

You are the landlord of your life and pain is that tenant who is destroying your building. "Building" is a metaphor for your dreams, goals, health, husband, children, or anything of value to you. We all know that by law there is a process that you must go through to evict someone from your property. There is a similar spiritual process associated with evicting pain. First, get its address. In order to be set free from anything negative you have to identify it and know where it lives in your life. In other words, where are its roots? Dig deeper than that cheating ex. We can't with straight faces continue to hold these men totally responsible for the messes of our lives. With that being said, "What happened in your past that made you weak enough to

settle for how he treated you or ignore the indicators

that he would be a cancer to your life?" My dear friend,

you have to get below the surface. In most cases, what

you are going through today is more a result of your

pain, not the cause.

**"…What does it profit a man to gain the whole
world and lose his soul?"**
Matthew 16:26

This is the hardest part of the process because you are

not only going to have to dig up those things that you

have tried to forget but you also have to accept

responsibility for the role you played in your own

struggles. This is not meant to make you feel bad; but

to jumpstart the process of soul-searching. Soul

searching is a close examination of yourself in an effort

to determine your true feelings, desires, and beliefs. Every woman should take this journey because our emotional nature has the tendency to blur the lines between what is important and what is mere "pomp and circumstance."

"It's Complicated"

Pain is a very complicated emotion and can be difficult to comprehend because its affects include some level of confusion and desperation, which are two common characteristics found in people that live in constant struggle. Yet, the same pain is filled with life lessons and strength, which are the companions of winners. An emotion with this type of complexity takes some getting to know.

You can't get to know pain until you are bettered

acquainted with yourself and the following survey has been developed with the intention of helping you gain clarity on your present state of being. Each question has a predetermined score based on your answer. The final score will give you a better idea of your mental-emotional state so you will be better able to navigate the path to your struggles' end.

Let's pray.

"Lord, it's in the name of Jesus that I ask you to give this woman the strength to go into the places of herself that she has tried to forget. Lord, I ask that fear be eliminated in her life because fear is an enemy of healing and your Word has taught us that fear is not in the vocabulary of your children. Lord, let every step that she takes toward restoration activate the blessings that she forfeited when she was trying to find herself. Lord, you know her and you know the traps that the enemy has planted in her life. I ask that you cover her and her family in the Blood of Jesus, and let every trap malfunction. Let her see this as evidence that she is not alone and that mercy is not a myth. Lord, I ask that you bind the spirit of confusion and replace it with the wisdom of the lessons she lost while she was going through. In Jesus name, Amen."

Mental-Emotional Check-Up

This survey is for your eyes only and the truth lies in your ability to be honest with yourself. This analysis is very important to your progress because, as my high school track coach would say, "You cannot catch what you cannot see!"

1. I believe that I have successfully overcome the trials I've faced throughout my life and I'm happy with where I am today.

(3) Agree   (2) Sometimes   (1) Disagree

2. I have allowed certain individuals to acquire and retain control of my life based on my experience with them.

(1) Agree   (2) Sometimes   (3) Disagree

3. I have set personal (self, love, family, friendships, etc.) and professional (school, work, etc.) goals and I have completed them.

(3) Agree   (2) Sometimes   (1) Disagree

4. I feel a strong sense of bitterness and anger about people and events in my life.

(1) Agree   (2) Sometimes   (3) Disagree

5. I have made vast improvements in my attitude within the past year and believe my personality has changed for the better.

(3) Agree **(2) Sometimes** **(1) Disagree**

6. I find it challenging to accept responsibility for my actions, even when it's clear that I have control over the situation.

(1) Agree **(2) Sometimes** **(3) Disagree**

7. I feel it's my responsibility to change the negative behaviors, thoughts, and practices in my life.

(3) Agree **(2) Sometimes** **(1) Disagree**

8. I am not open to asking for help or input from others unless they have experienced what I am going through.

(1) Agree **(2) Sometimes** **(3) Disagree**

9. If everyone who has hurt me came back and apologized, I would accept their apology.

(3) Agree   **(2) Perhaps**   **(1) Disagree**

10. I believe the negative cycle in my life is unbreakable.

(1) Agree   **(2) Sometimes**   **(3) Disagree**

11. I take my negative experiences and turn them into opportunities of positive personal growth.

(3) Agree   **(2) Sometimes**   **(1) Disagree**

12. When I look at myself, I don't like what I see.

(1) Agree   **(2) Sometimes**   **(3) Disagree**

13. I quickly seek to resolve problems with others before the problem consumes me.

(3) Agree   **(2) Sometimes**   **(1) Disagree**

14. I feel like my personality, energy, and

behavior has a negative effect on those around me.

(1) Agree   (2) Sometimes   (3) Disagree

Starting with the first question, add up the number

beside your answer choices and place your total in the

blank below.   Please see the result summary on the

next page.   **Total:** _____

Summary of Results

(14-23) "Headed for Self Destruction" - This category signifies that you are in a stage of your life where you don't like yourself very much and you are feeling extremely vulnerable. For the most part, your outlook of yourself is negative and you are screaming for help, but it feels like no one is coming to your aid. You have closed the door to healing and have accepted the state that you are in as permanent.

(24-33) "Emotionally Content" - This category signifies that you are in a place of comfort and don't seek to reach far beyond the basic reassurance of who you are. You are in denial about some of the things that have a major effect on you, but have addressed most of your key issues. You aim to blend in with the majority and avoid showing too much emotion when it comes to certain matters. You have become a better judge of the company you keep, but you are finding it difficult to shake negative relationships. Your new positive awareness and negative surroundings keep you in a place of unrest and as a result you have an unexplained emptiness.

(34-42) "Emotionally Prosperous" - This category signifies that you know your worth! You may have been broken, beaten, and torn emotionally, but you have not allowed it to conquer your peace and happiness. The obstacles you've faced have made you stronger and you are not ashamed to share your experiences with others in an effort to help them overcome, as well. Some may say that you have a strong personality because they don't know your story. Your journey has not been easy, but you work daily on becoming a better person.

"And the LORD answered me, and said, Write the vision, and make it plain upon tables, so he may run that reads it"

Habakkuk 2:2

Don't get discouraged by the results; it's more important that you know where to start. Even if you find that you are on the right track there is still room to grow. Lastly, let pain know that you will be repairing your "property" immediately! Let her know that she should pack her bags because you will no longer respect her presence. Now, write down every hindrance in your life and don't omit those things that pain might not know belong to her (bad habits, attitudes, nagging thoughts, people etc.). A hindrance is anything that makes it difficult for you to be productive and live in peace and happiness.

1) _____

2) _____

3) _____

4) _____

5) _____

You have just mentally and physically put an identification number on everything in your life that is fueling your suffering. Pain that is unidentified or ignored quietly eases its way into your decision-making process, introducing struggle into your life. Struggle is a by-product of pain and if it is allowed to move freely it will place restrictions on your quality of life. If you ever intend to meet goals and maintain some sense of peace and happiness you have to take control of the pain you feel. Will pain ever completely disappear? The answer is no in many instances. It is a constant battle, but the goal is that it does not handicap your present and future well-being. This list should be placed on your bathroom mirror, steering wheel, or anywhere that gives you daily access to it. Be patient with yourself, you did not acquire these strongholds overnight, and it might take some time to completely eliminate them. Although, it is important to remember that "the longer they stay the longer you pay."

The Roots

The Two Faces of Pain

Pain is pain, right? It all feels the same, but my experiences have taught me that it has at least two faces: the pain that accompanies misfortune and the pain associated with trouble. Misfortune represents the suffering that is beyond your control. Nothing you did caused it; it just happened. Trouble, on the other hand, is the suffering you bring on yourself.

3 MISFORTUNE-GOD'S TOUGH LOVE

"...what we suffer now is nothing compared to the glory he will reveal to us later."

Romans 8:18

Misfortune, commonly known as "bad luck," refers to unfortunate circumstances or events in life that leave you confused and miserable. This could be anything as great as the death of a loved one or something as trivial as your physical appearance. These circumstances leave you thinking, Life is not fair! Oh, but it is. We will all have our share of problems, but it's our reactions to them that determine the depths of our struggles. You are going to have to master the art of "falling down and getting up again." So as long as you can breathe, life is pretty fair, but you cheat yourself when you fall down and stay there.

You have to accept the fact that nobody's exempt from

misfortune. There are some people that will try to lead you to believe that their life is perfect, and I am not blaming them for portraying it, but you for believing it. Anybody that tells you they have not gone through anything is either too immature to know the difference or one of the biggest liars in world. Each of us will experience ups and downs, and misfortunes are God's built-in "downers." God knows the challenges you will face in life and misfortunes are custom-built simulators designed specifically to build the strength you will need to endure those things that are necessary for growth; teach you to avoid things you cannot handle; prepare you for the unavoidable; and, ultimately to humble you to a place where you have compassion for other people in situations similar to those that he will teach you to overcome. God doesn't want to see you suffer, but as a parent one of his responsibilities is to make sure that you can take care of yourself and misfortune is his training ground.

WORDS OF WINNING ~~WISDOM~~

"There will come a time in life when all you will have is God and yourself, and misfortunes are designed to make sure you understand that this is more than enough."

Misfortunes are some of the most powerful change-agents in the world. It can make the worst woman change for the better and the best woman throw her life away. You will be better prepared to respond to misfortune if you accept the fact that in life you will go through setbacks and it will hurt, period. I know that might seem blunt, but understanding this is the difference between folding under the pressure and being open to the possibility that hard times might have positive purpose.

Some awful things just happen. Death is the greatest example. It is the cycle of life. No one lives forever, we all have to leave this world sometime or another, and as a result we are going to lose some loved ones. Will it hurt? Of course. Can you give up on life because of it? NO! Some of us dwell too long on who we've lost instead of living for who we have left. God still has a purpose and plan for your life.

Death is one of those things you will never be prepared for, but you have to fight through it. No matter how much it hurts you have to get up every day after the fact and operate as normal as possible. I am not telling you not to grieve, but you cannot get lost in your emotions.

God has given each of us the built-in power to

overcome what we cannot control, but you have to rest

on his Word and keep pushing. My mother said it best,

"It is alright to cry and to be sad, but don't cry as if

there is no hope."

4 TROUBLE –SELF INFLICTED WOUNDS

"The wisest of women builds her house, but folly with her own hands tears it down."

Proverbs 14:1

If we would just accept misfortunes as life's learning curves we wouldn't suffer as many self-inflicted wounds. From the moment misfortune crashes into our lives it is human nature to experience mental and emotional distress (depression, anxiety, sadness, anger etc.). These emotions wake you up in the morning and put you to bed at night. This consistency can quickly frustrate you and if you focus on your feelings hopelessness will start to show its ugly head. We all know that a woman that buys the idea that there is no hope is a woman that does not believe she can be helped, and in walks trouble. A mentally healthy woman would never place herself in harm's way, but a troubled woman loses the natural impulse to preserve herself. Self-preservation is the instinct to act in your own best interest and to ensure your survival. The first law of self-preservation is to "take care of yourself," and if you allow worthlessness to take root your body and soul will have no defense against the evils of the world. You will stop filtering your activities and every move you make will be in an effort to remedy the pain you feel and consequence will soon make her grand entrance.

Will you wrestle or withdraw?

When life happens, as women we fall in one of two categories: we either wrestle or withdraw! The wrestler is in a tug-of-war with her emotions and "the right thing to do." The withdrawer on the other hand, has completely given in to her own negative desires and she

allows the truth to become whatever helps her cope

from day-to-day. Let's start with the withdrawer. She

lives and dies by her emotions. She does what she wants

to do with little or no regard to the effects it could have

on her life because subconsciously she has given up

hope. This woman has let her life's trials turn her every

which way but loose. Many women would deny that

they fall into this category, but their actions scream the

total opposite.

WORDS OF WINNING WISDOM

We have to become aware of the fact that our <u>actions</u> not our <u>mouths</u> tell our truths.

The withdrawer's actions are also indicative of an

estranged relationship with God. She has secretly lost faith in his willingness or ability to make her life better. Many women won't verbally admit that they no longer trust God, but if you *feel* it he can *hear* it loud and clear. Stop for a second and ask yourself, "Do I truly believe that God will make **(insert your greatest struggle)** better? Take a few deep breathes, in through your nose out through your mouth, and then let your heart speak. If the answer is not 100% yes you need to analyze yourself, get to the core of the disconnect, research it, and resolve it. The lack of trust that we develop is one of Satan's best kept secrets because trust and faith have the exact same meaning. If you tell someone "I don't trust you!" it's the same as saying "I don't have faith in you." This could prove to be the reason that many of your prayers have gone

unanswered.

"Life is a Heavy Weight Fight"

The wrestler, on the other hand, leads a very

inconsistent life. One minute she strives for a better and

the next second she is making decisions that could

possibly destroy everything she was initially trying to

build. This tug-of-war represents the growth process

and is healthy to a certain extent, but there is not much

wiggle room. The wiggle room represents God's grace

period and during this time you are protected from

consequence. This is his way of saying, "I understand

that you are hurting and I know many of your sins are

just a desperate attempt to deal with pain of those

things that you have no control over. So, I am going to

delay consequence and send as many warnings signals as I can in hopes that you will identify and correct the 'error' of your own ways."

"No matter what life throws at you, don't let it knock you any further than your knees."

My grandmother, Mable Lean gave me this very valuable advice. Ladies, it's time that we lay down the victim's (or Woe is me) mindset and explore the characteristics of a victor. The victor's "luck," in many instances, is worse than the victim's, but instead of "giving up" the victor says to herself, "Life is testing me again, but the best of me lies in my ability to stay focused and keep my emotions in check." If you are in a healthy state of mind you have been both of these women (a victim and a victor). Although, it will take some serious soul-searching to completely understand this. The victim in me blamed my lack-luster existence on my setbacks and the people in my life that hurt me. However, as the victor in me matured, I realized that these things didn't have the ability to destroy me, but through my reactions I could destroy myself.

We have to live "strong" in spite of difficult people and circumstances. The truth is some of the things you suffered weren't punishment or God's lack of love for you (which by the way is impossible); it's just life! And you can no longer allow life to get in the way of living. I know firsthand how life's curveballs can knock you to your knees, but it is what you do while you're down there and how you operate when you get up that determines your tomorrow, not the curveball itself.

5 CHOICE-LIFE'S STEERING WHEEL

"Choice will determine whether life's journey is smooth or rocky, if your next stop is a peaceful place or one filled with chaos, and most importantly it will determine the depth of your struggle."

I know what you are thinking, I didn't have a choice; you don't know what I've been through! I don't know what you have been through, but I am sure you had a choice. **You had at least two options, either:**

- Hold on to your hurts and allow them to be a constant source of struggle in your life

Or

- Snatch the lesson these painful events were designed to teach and move on from it.

I know firsthand how difficult it can be to find the energy to stay positive and focused when you are carrying life's struggles on your back. However, God has sent us a saving grace that is designed to protect us

when we are blinded by the sweat of our burdens.

Allow me to formally introduce you to choice. It is the

remedy to humble beginnings and can fill the day after a

bad situation with promise. When life knocks the wind

out of you, choice, if used correctly, allows you to

gracefully pick yourself up, dust yourself off, and keep

moving forward.

"Look Before You Leap"

Have you ever wondered why some women find

success in life and others don't? The reason is not as

complicated as you think. Although, I need you to think

beyond financial and professional success, but also

include your private and personal desires. Productive

women have developed the understanding that poor

decision-making can ruin even the best intentions. You know that good-hearted, wholesome woman that always falls for the "low-life" man or that great mother with bad habits. These women have the heart to do the right thing, but make horrible choices. If we want to change the trajectory of our lives we have to start weighing the pros and cons in every circumstance. The Pros represent the advantages of a decision and the cons represent the disadvantages. I know what you are thinking, "This is not living! Who wants to walk around always over-thinking every decision they make!" Winners that's who. When our sisters get to the winners' circle we have tendency to be blinded by their glory when our focus should be their stories. Every woman that has ever had a successful career, marriage, family etc. and got there with her virtue intake has made a lot of sacrifices and shed a lot tears. She set standards and goals for herself and lived on purpose more so than pleasure. While you were having "fun" she was "focused" and now she has pleasures that "the world didn't give and can't take away."

Women with sustainable peace and happiness rarely make **popular** decisions, but **purposed** decisions. A purposed woman's decisions are very calculated and have little or nothing to do with temporary satisfaction. If you could hear her thoughts when she is faced with a potentially destructive situation she is asking herself, "Will action 'A' get me to destination 'Z' safely, with my goals met, and my well-being intact?"

"The Power to Choose"

Choice is not only a power we all possess, but one of God's greatest gifts. Choice gives us the power to overcome our beginnings, our mistakes, and our struggles. You are probably thinking, I didn't choose this life it chose me! Are you sure? Because I agree with the fact that we can't choose our beginnings, but the ending is a choice. "Will there be some bumps in the road?" Sure, but the only way they can stop you is if you quit, and by quit I mean start giving up what's right for wrong.

If you ever intended to accomplish and **maintain** anything worthwhile you have to make good decisions. The life you will ultimately live is not dictated by the family you are born into, the environment you grew up in, or by what happens to you, but more by your will to

succeed, your work ethic, and how well you choose!

6 IS HEALING THE ROAD LESS TRAVELED?

"He said to her, "Daughter, your faith has healed you. Go in peace and be freed from your suffering."

Mark 5: 34

The year was 1999. I had just played in an all-star basketball game for the entire state of Mississippi, but had no scholarship offer to continue my education. Statistically, players far less talented were moving on to four year colleges and I didn't understand why I had been overlooked. An old man that followed my team stopped me after the game and said, "You are a great athlete with a horrible attitude and this is the reason you will have to pay for the rest of your education."

Of course, I gave him "a piece of my mind," but he just looked at me like someone watching a wounded animal. I saw pity in his eyes which infuriated me. I was angry, but not at him, at myself. That was the first time someone I considered an outsider saw through my tough exterior. His eyes told me that he knew something far deeper than scholarship was haunting me. I worked very hard to cope with the pain of my past. Basketball kept me sane, but at that moment I realized that I no longer had that safe haven. So I took to prayer and it was quickly revealed to me that my long term goal should not have been to cope, but to heal. Coping, by definition, is to deal effectively with something difficult; whereas healing is the process of repair. Ask yourself, "Do I want to *deal* or *heal?*" Basketball was not a poor coping mechanism, it was just not enough. Many of our coping mechanisms provide temporary relief, but do not offer any real remedy. It's similar to putting pressure on a gunshot wound; it might temporarily stop the bleeding, but you're still shot. Without further medical care this wound could prove fatal to your physical health. We need to apply the same urgency and in many cases the same process to our mental-emotional health.

Like every other adult with struggles; I pretended they didn't exist. However, my decisions (at some level) were still fueled by them. People process pain differently; mine made me angry and very determined. I had the worst attitude in the world and I was not afraid of anybody. However, I took every opportunity to aid the underdog. I know this does not line up with the characteristics of most angry people, but this is where I hid my fundamental need. When I was suffering I felt nobody came to my rescue.

"Time Does Not Heal Emotional Wounds"

Contrary to popular belief, emotional wounds are not healed with time, but time does more damage. The older we get the more freedom we gain and freedom to a broken person is a license to self-destruct. As we get older, instead of having tantrums and crying tears we become bad parents and even worse people. "I'm grown" becomes the blanket statement for everything negative in our lives. The naked truth is that if you have not done the spiritual, mental, and emotional work necessary to shed the pain you have experienced it is still present and hindering you from being your personal best. My emotional pain cost me my talent and about $40,000(in student loans.)

"Addiction"

There is a darker side to emotional injury. Many people choose poor coping mechanisms and become addicted to the affects. Addiction is the strong and harmful need to regularly have or do something. Men, wine, excessive food, laziness, are a few poor coping mechanisms common to women. If you find comfort in positive things you might lose some battles, but you can still win the war. However, if your coping mechanisms even have the potential to harm you; you can quickly go from losing to being lost. The baby's attraction to the pacifier is a great illustration of this. Babies gravitate to pacifiers because it soothes them, but they are unconscious to the fact that they are getting nothing lasting out of the experience. By the time the baby realizes she is not being "fed" she is addicted to the soothing affect.

"HELP!"

You have to decide that you will no longer be an active member of your own destruction and start backing away from the negativity in your life. If you can quit cold turkey, more power to you, but there is no shame in asking for help (God, counseling, coaching, etc.). I know many people think that counseling is for the crazy which is untrue, but I would rather people think I am crazy for going than to know I am crazy when I am skipping around wearing a mink in May. Although, I am joking some of us have strongholds that secretly have us close to the edge. Counselors and coaches merely help bring clarity to your confusion.

My Life's Purpose

I knew that helping people was a part of God's plan for my life because every time I met someone that was going through a hard time I would almost uncontrollably pour everything I could think of into them. My efforts were rejected many times because to many people it was unrealistic for someone to care that much about a complete stranger.

A few years ago, I was in a grocery store and as I was shopping I notice this teenager stuffing food into his jacket. I watched him for a few minutes because I wanted to make sure my eyes weren't deceiving me. He was stealing. As I walked closer to him I realized he was homeless. He was about 17 years old, with tangled hair, and wearing a very long, dirty coat. I walked up to him and with a smile said, "Can I pay for your food?" He looked at me and immediately pulled out a pen and piece of paper and began writing. "I can't talk," he said. He also wrote "Yes, can I get a few more thing?" I respond "yes" and off we went.

I followed him around the store until he finished. When we got to the register the cashier just looked at me like I'd lost my mind. I paid for his things, asked the cashier for her pen, and on the back of his receipt I wrote, "God loves you and so do I. Hang in there." I hugged him, gave him the money I had in my purse, and he walked away. The cashier was in complete disbelief.

I love people and I have a special affection for those that are hurting. As a result, I decided to become a life coach. I literally cried through much of the training and

I am sure the other participants were wondering "What's wrong with her?" They were tears of joy. It felt amazing to finally have the tools necessary to effectively fulfill the will of God for my life. Life has a way of breaking us down and life coaches are trained to help you pick up the pieces. The coach cannot tell anyone who you are or your personal business and if you keep your mouth closed and your mind open, the world will only see your transformation not your process.

Contrary to popular belief, we also have each other. You are suffering in silence when your "sister" is holding your healing! She might be your mother, coworker, friend, or a stranger, but one of her assignments in life is you. She is strong, wise, "if she can't help you she won't hurt you", and most importantly she has "been there, done that." She will

give you comfort in knowing that there is virtue in

patience and power in prayer. Now you can't tell

everybody your business so be careful. Some of us are

as messy as mud pies. However, this woman will be

your personal secret keeper, but you won't recognize

her until you make change a priority.

FIGHTING TEMPTATIONS

7 FIGHTING TEMPTATIONS

No temptation has overtaken you that is not common to man. God is faithful, and he will not let you be tempted beyond your ability, but with the temptation he will also provide the way of escape, that you may be able to endure it."

1 Corinthians 10:13

Even when you put your emotions in a chokehold you will always be tested and if you don't become your own gatekeeper there are negative forces that can send you headfirst back into your old ways or worse! The strongest women fall prey to temptation; however, 1 Corinthians 10:13 makes it clear that you have everything you need to fight, but you have to be strategic. Satan is the puppet master of all temptation and he will attack the very areas of your life that you are

61

weak in, so plan your attack!

Strategy 1: Mind over Matter

First things first, you have to get your mind right.

This is the simplest, most complicated decision you

will ever make. If you have had the opportunity to

discuss the intimate details of anyone's success they all

make reference to their thought process. The mind is

the garden of all actions and you have to nurture the

positive thoughts (flowers) and pull out the negatives

(weeds). Explore the positives they will blossom into

blessings. However, weeds are poisonous, they taste

bad, and have thorns or other physical features that

make them difficult to remove. These characteristics are

also symbolic of your negative thoughts. If you let them

linger too long they have the means to destroy you.

When negative thoughts cross your mind quickly redirect them with something positive. **Here are a few examples:**

Negative Thought: "I didn't get that job because I am not good enough."

Positive Thought: "I didn't get that job because the same stresses that I have at my current position will be magnified there. God knows my prayers and they won't be answered there."

Negative Thought: "He left me because she looks better than me."

Positive Thought: "He left me because I was disobedient. God revealed his short-comings to me shortly after we met and I ignored his warning. I

suffered by association.

Strategy 2: Arm Yourself with Standards

Standards are the evidence of a "made up mind." Many

of us have adopted standards, but whether we use them

depends on the mood we are in or the people we are

around. It is not until a healthy mental state collaborates

with self-control are standards most effective. Standards

also protect you from the vultures of the world. A great

example is a mother that never allows dates to meet her

children or the single woman that has decided to be

celibate. Standards keep risk low and protection high.

Standards also derail most hasty decisions. You know

the ones we only become conscious of after the fact.

God has very strong feelings about hastiness and this is

made clear in Proverbs 6:16, which reads: "There are six things the Lord hates, seven that are detestable to him…feet that are quick to rush into evil." I was sold at the word "hate." Think about something you hate. You don't want anything to do with it or be around it. I don't know about you, but I cannot afford for God to lose interest in me. This scripture indicates that when you know better and do wrong God is offended. He is disgusted by the fact that you are ignoring the lessons he has taught you and this scripture is simply saying "consider yourself warned."

Strategy 3: Get in Direct Communication with God

The realization that God hated my approach to sin gave me insight into why many of my struggles seemed to last forever. I broke it and he didn't fix it. I am sure he wanted to, because no parent wants to see their child suffer. However, a good parent understands that some of the best lessons are bought. For years, I rode the rollercoaster of bad decisions; suffering consequences, and then crying to God for forgiveness and relief. It wasn't until I coupled my prayers with meditation did I realize it was my personal responsibility to make many of my wrongs right. When we go to God in prayer we do the talking, but when we meditate God speaks. Meditation is simply quiet time with God. However, be mindful of the fact that God is a gentlemen and many people miss his message because while he is "whispering" guidance, pain is "screaming." This is why daily meditation is important, you learn through repetition to recognize the voice of God no matter how noisy life gets.

"The Funeral Arrangements"

If you are "sick and tired of being sick and tired," prove it! Make some funeral

arrangements! Let me be more specific. It is now time for you to take your new awareness and put the causes of your struggles to bed. This includes those people, places, and things that you know have the tendency to bring the worst out of you. I am not trying to encourage you to destroy anything or anybody, but I am encouraging you to bury their influence in your life. Satan's objective has always been to take what you value, kill your spirit, and destroy your life, but it's your responsibility to stop giving him the satisfaction. In the following chapters we will take a long, hard look at the common causes of constant struggle.

8 THE BLAME GAME

"As long as it's some else's fault where you are is where you will be."

You can give up ever moving forward if you don't give up blaming other people or things for the struggles in your life. Maybe they did hurt you, but they can't heal you. You've heard the cliché "hurt people, hurt people." So how can you possibly expect that broken person to fix you? I always told myself "the person that harmed me is the one with the issues; it's not my fault and as a result it's not my issue to hold on to. Yes it hurts, but I am stronger than what I've been through!" You also have to become aware of the fact that blame protects the pain in your life. Think about it. Overtime it's human nature to become numb to the physical effects of what a person or event did to you, but blame fuels these events by keeping them relevant in your mind and these thoughts are constantly reactivating your emotions. This is too much power to give anyone or anything.

Blame is an extremely unhealthy dwelling place and those of us that take up residence here are stuck waiting for a miracle or for someone to give us closure when healing is a personal responsibility.

WORDS OF WINNING WISDOM

"Stop crying over spilled milk or waiting for an apology you don't need it; emotional healing is a personal, very private journey by design."

I learned this extremely valuable lesson in a conversation I had with God in my early twenties. One day I asked him, "Why is my life one hard time after the other?" A small voice said "YOU!" "You are the common denominator in every situation you find yourself in!" At the time I did not completely understand this because I felt powerless to many of the things that were going on around me. I had suffered indirectly by the actions of others and I reacted negatively because I didn't know what to do with the discomfort I felt. Hindsight being 20/20, I brainwashed myself into believing that God accepted my wrong doing because of what I went through. Everything I did was a desperate attempt to medicate the pain I felt. I was deep in the confines of my victim's mindset and stayed dressed for a pity party.

The Pity Party

The pity party is the timeframe between a painful event and our ability to let go and move forward. During this time our lives are at a stand-still because we spend most of our time feeling sorry for ourselves. The "pity party" is the mind's unhealthy approach to healing emotional pain. During the pity party the mind is on auto-pilot and your emotions are in the driver's seat. When your emotions operate alone your days are reduced to thoughts of revenge, anger, sadness, and worthlessness. Snap out of it! Nothing is still hurt but your feelings and I don't know about you, but my feelings are done cheating me out of my destiny! You have already been beaten up by the events in your life that caused the pain and you can't afford to let pity finish the job.

"The Chain Reaction"

You will know when you've overcome blame, because you will begin to feel empathy for the person that hurt you in spite of what they've done. These feelings will stem from your understanding that their behavior is only a chain reaction of their own suffering. Even with this understanding you have to work through your own wounds. So take that "woe is me" energy and channel it into something positive. I got an advanced degree, started a small business, and even wrote this book.

9 THE MISCONCEPTION OF THE MISTAKE
"Oops Again?"

Think back over your life. How many of your "mistakes" actually were? Truth be told, the first time you indulged in the negative behavior "might" have been a mistake, but every time after that was definitely a choice. The reason is because by definition mistakes are errors in judgment, action, or belief; however, trial, error, observation, and reflection have gifted you with awareness. So as an adult woman, if you can't pinpoint your wrong doing 99.9% of the time then I'm the tooth fairy.

The mistake was initially intended to describe a misstep never to be easily repeated, but unwed pregnancy, adultery etc. have become more common associations

74

of the word. It has become the scapegoat people use to soften the blows that their inappropriate behaviors have on their reputations and their relationships. Many people have brainwashed themselves into believing that if they use the word that somehow they will be exempt from consequence, but wake up! You are still left holding the bag your loved ones are just holding it with you.

"Don't Love Me to Death"

"Everybody makes mistakes" is the tagline for most self-destructive people. They know its kryptonite to many of their loved ones, which is why it is so popular. We have all preyed on our family members and friends at some point in our lives. And although they won't admit it, they have contributed to our self-destruction.

They cosigned for or ignored our bad habits, all in the name of love. The most visible demonstration of this is the relationship between parents and children. Some mothers will make excuses to the end for their children. Someone can tell you that your child robbed a food bank and your response will be, "He shouldn't go to jail because that food was free!" Seriously, why do we do this? Deep down you know you are not helping your child. You have to realize that what you are portraying as protection they are digesting as escape. I have a theory that maybe a mother's motivation is deeper than the obvious. Maybe she needs to believe that her child is not capable of certain behaviors because it could serve as a reflection of her own flaws. Meditate on that and then get over yourself! Your child's life could

depend on it.

"Thank God Almost Doesn't Count"

A Poem

Why did God choose me to be born into this misery?

My parents are so caught in their own lives that they didn't even see me.

They feed, clothe, work and provide,

But never nurture or confide.

As a result I have grown into a young woman with a fragmented view

Of the right and the wrong thing to do.

They didn't realize that I would mimic their mistakes,

And when they became aware it was "almost" too late.

I was living their lifestyles and not the lessons they taught

And unfortunately for me my lessons were bought.

"Almost is the operative word because a stranger introduced me to my worth and I am no longer captive to the life of my birth.

10 Family

"The Ties that Bind"

We have become too comfortable blaming society's dysfunctions on our school systems and the economy when the naked truth is that it is largely associated with the breakdown of the family. Moreover, many of our own personal failures are a result of the poor influences of some of our loved ones. The family is the foundation of our individual development and growth (physical, mental, spiritual, and emotional), and many of us are unconscious to the fact that our personal negatives are a direct result of how we were raised. Family is "an association of people who share common beliefs and activities," and you have to get to the place where you are selective about what you choose to believe.

WORDS OF ~~WISDOM~~ WINNING

"Many women have undergone lifelong struggles because they mimicked their mothers."

"Hard Questions"

I am convinced that all parents love their children and want what's best for them, but I'm also certain that a parent's ability to love and protect cannot extend beyond their own prior knowledge and experiences. In other words, they cannot give you what they don't have! You have to get out of that "family to a fault" mindset and become independent in the way you consume information. Ask yourself questions such as, "How much of what I was taught was:

• Appropriate?

• A result of the elders in my family not knowing any better?"

I realize that these are hard questions, but I also need you to realize that many of the struggles that are commonplace in your life are a direct result of you operating on this information. No matter how much you love your family members, the fact is that nobody's perfect and this includes some of their beliefs and viewpoints. It can be difficult for the elders in your family to advise on the "right thing to do" when sometimes they are not familiar with it themselves; moreover, the truth could expose their shortcomings. Take a long hard look at your advisors (family members, friends, etc.).

• Are they qualified to give you advice?

• Do their actions and the results of those actions replicate your goals?

Remember this information is not intended to give you permission to be disrespectful, just selective. You have to become a better consumer of life and not so quick to "buy" everything people are "selling," no matter who it is! If the information you receive does not line up with God's law regarding what's "right" then it is "wrong."

"Perfect People Be Quiet"

We are all flawed and no one is going to admit or tell you everything they've done wrong. However, if your advisors always paint themselves perfect and never share their weaknesses; they might be too proud to be honest and as a result you have to second-guess everything they say. You need an advisor that will tell you what is right, even if it exposes their wrongs. Take any advice you are not sure about into your prayer time because even when a person has the best intentions it is merely their interpretation of the truth, and it might not be the best application for your life.

INDEPENDENCE

We have to learn to base our acceptance of information on the "content" not the "character." The next question, although very controversial, is one that we all have to ask ourselves: "Are you willing to forfeit the life God intended for you to have in the name of family?" My intention is not to destroy your family, but give you the equipment you need to become an independent thinker. God honors family which makes this a very delicate subject. Yet, he also gave each of us a brain and you have to choose your own path.

This is not an easy task because "the right way" oftentimes means turning a deaf ear to people that indulge in behaviors that you need to avoid or are trying to eliminate from your life. Although, you are not alone. God is just a prayer away and eventually the family members you feel you lost in this process will be attracted to your transformation. It's at that moment that you will possess the power of influence! This power will give you their attention and when that time comes, share with them the blueprint that God gave you.

WORDS OF WINNING ~~WISDOM~~

"Whatever a family celebrates is where it excels!"

As a woman, you will become the standard for your household. Men have a huge responsibility as well, but that's another book. I want you to understand your role in the family. Do you know that everything you do wrong affects everyone under your roof? It either confuses them or encourages bad behavior? The cliché "Do what I say and not what I do" did not work when your parents said it to you and it won't work with your children either.

Children should never be privy to adult activities. You're struggling as a result of your lifestyle choices so why would you want to plant those seeds of suffering in them. Children idolize their mothers and will do anything for them, even mimic their behavior when deep down they know it's wrong. Your children would rather adopt your bad habits than deal with the idea that you are not a good person.

"Fatherless Daughters"

A Poem

Did your father abandon his role in your life or

Pass away before you were ready?

Either way I know you feel empty

And sometimes unsteady.

Have you dated secretly trying to fill this void?

Has your broken heart been misinterpreted as wild?

Too embarrassed just to admit you're a fatherless child.

These relationships have done a number on your self-

esteem,

But these guys weren't trying to be mean.

You gave; they took that doesn't make them a crook.

Let's take a closer look.

You tried to fill holes in your heart with pieces that

didn't fit

Your father wasn't there that's it.

Please don't take that statement wrong.

I know it seems a little strong.

But we like to paint life with our emotions and not the truth.

Roaming aimlessly looking for proof

When the truth is just the truth.

Some things won't have the ending you want,

Just take what you need and leave what you don't.

Make sure his absence does not leave you reduced,

You know less than your best, isolated, a recluse.

Look into his history his reason for leaving will no longer be a mystery.

People can only give what they have

And his absence might not make sense to you,

But I guarantee if he couldn't handle it neither could you.

God will fill every void you ever had, and although you didn't have a father you definitely have a dad.

11 FRIENDS

"Walk with the wise and become wise, for a companion of fools suffers harm."

Proverbs 13:20

Peer pressure is a childish gesture to many adults and somehow when we become women we grow out of it. Stop kidding yourself! You are just as vulnerable to it now as you were when you were 16 years old. It's human nature! You cannot hang around a person or group of people for a prolonged period of time and not adopt (whether consciously or unconsciously) some of their habits and activities. We are very naïve to this fact and as a result some of our girlfriends are partially responsible for the struggles in our lives. I know many of you are thinking, "Nobody makes me to do anything. Everything I do or don't do is because I want to!" And you are correct! It's the person's lifestyle choices that plant seeds of negativity in your life.

"Are You Socially Healthy?"

Think about your circle of friends (this includes boyfriends) and think about their personalities and habits. Are these associations healthy? Keep in mind that I am not only referring to who they have been to you; I am speaking to who they are to themselves. You have to realize that if a person mistreats themselves they do not have the ability to treat you any better. You have to decide if your "good" friend with "bad" habits is worth your quality of life. I am not telling you to disown them, but you have to identify what's more important, their friendship or your well-being. Sounds over the top, right? However, it's a trade many of us are unconsciously making. Our relationships always pose one of the biggest threats to our well-being.

Where Do Your Loyalties Lie?"

I know it's beginning to seem as though you have to give up everything and everybody to grow, but it's more about taking control of yourself, which includes identifying temptations and the people associated with them. The first thing you have to do is be honest with your friends about who you are trying to become and what you are trying to do. This is the process of, in my Grandmother Sally's voice of, "separating the wheat from the weeds" (Mathew 13: 24-32).

In this process you will separate your real from your fair-weather (or fake) friends.

A real friend will respect your decision to change, even

if they do not choose to. However, your fair-weather (fake) friends are only there if you do what they do. Your fake friends will try to persuade you not to change or tease you for the notion. When this takes place you have a decision to make either maintain the relationship or grow into the person God designed you to be. You cannot have both. We all have that girlfriend whose vices could destroy everything that works well in our lives. They are members of Satan's wrecking crew and their lifestyles choices are designed to take you off the right path. This makes me think about married women with single friends. The single friend still wants you to go to the *same* places and hang with the *same* people you did when you were single. She gets upset saying things like, "You've changed," or she makes you feel bad simply because you make decisions that honor the commitment you made to your husband. I am not saying that married and single women cannot be friends, but unless the friendship is genuine and there is a mutual respect for each other's state of being these relationships can be difficult. The single friend has to respect the marriage and the married friend has to respect the single friend's freedom.

Intertwined Destinies

As you stand at these crossroads, remember prolonged associations oftentimes intertwine destinies. In other words, if you make decisions to maintain unhealthy relationships you could quite possibly share consequences or even worse, take one for the team. Those that choose to maintain these relationships, even after it becomes clear they are unhealthy, are commonly known as followers. The follower's behavior is fueled by his or her own inadequacies or misfortunes. There is a sad story in the shadows of every follower. Unfortunately, followers rarely "live happily ever after" because, instead of fighting to overcome their own shortcomings they are fighting the effects of artificial "fillers" or "friends." Followers have a tendency to do whatever is necessary (whether right or wrong) to feel a part of something or someone. We have enough to overcome in this life all on our own; we do not need the influence of bad company. The absolute worst decision a follower can make is to associate with individuals with bad and destructive habits. Instinctively, we all have traits of a follower, because it's easier and more comfortable to stay confined to a group than to stand alone. Let's focus on the latter. Usually the person that chooses to stand alone does so because the group's activities pose a threat to her well-being. The comfort once found in the group is no longer present. This person is very aware of the social consequences tied to walking away, but knows that the personal stakes are entirely too high to stay.

The Exit Strategy

Analyze your friends. If their habits, lifestyles, or personalities could have an adverse effect on your well-being (freedom, safety, health, goals, etc.), prepare your exit. This is not the easiest thing to do, but it's impossible to clean yourself up without cleaning up your surroundings. It's best to be straight forward and honest with them; any other approach is way too complicated.

Here are a few examples of ways to start this conversation:

"I love you to death, but I can't get caught up in **(insert negative behavior here)** anymore because I plan to **(insert goals)**. "We have had some good times, but you know I am trying to do **(insert goals here),** and I can't hang out with you guys anymore when you **(insert negative behavior here)**.

These conversations will almost always reveal who your real friends are. **You will receive some variation of one the following responses:**

1. **"If you are scared, say you're scared!"** This fair-weather friend has sold out to negativity and will

have nothing to do with you if you do not engage in it with them. Cut all ties with this person and run as fast as you can. This person is the toughest to walk away from because most of the time this is the leader of your social group and the majority of your friends are tied to her (or him).

2. **"Okay, but change is not for me."** This person is the most dangerous because they care about you as a person, but will not refrain from the behavior in your presence. We struggle with being loyal to this person. Loyalty is a feeling or attitude of devoted attachment and affection. The person that uses the word "loyalty" or any other with the same meaning is the master and trying to make you the puppet. How backwards is it to be loyal to a friend that has habits

that could destroy you and her? This person understands your need for change, but will not put your wishes over their own vices.

3.   **"I understand."** This person is genuine and you should invite them to start the journey with you. This very direct response lends to the idea that they have been thinking about change as well. However, if at any time they become more of a hindrance than a help you have to limit your association with them too. But reassure them that when you find yourself you won't forget about them. You cannot allow yourself to get sucked back in by anyone.

The following is list of characteristics that I look for in choosing friendships:

Ambition - They have to have goals. If they don't have

goals they will not respect mine.

Leaders - Followers tend to have a lot of baggage. I don't need anybody else's bad habits. I have a hard enough time wrestling with my own.

Honesty - I don't need co-signers as friends; I need people around me that are not afraid to tell me the truth. Co-signers will stand by and let you ruin your life in the name of friendship.

Level-Headed - These people have similar characteristics to leaders, but they have one characteristic that some leaders do not have. They always remain true to who they are. They cannot be easily persuaded to do wrong. They are usually very strong willed and focused. All of their actions are calculated and they always begin with the end in mind.

Spiritual - You have to have a relationship with God, period. This is most important.

These are only a few of the characteristics I look for in friends, but nobody's perfect and we cannot choose all of our relationships (professional, relatives etc.), but I can choose when and how I associate with them. Be very observant and pick out each person's unhealthy habits and put those on your list of things not to do!

12 POOR SELF PORTRAIT

"........for I am fearfully and wonderfully made:
marvelous are your works; and that my soul knows
right well."

Psalms 139:14

If you cannot recite this scripture with confidence and
feel good about yourself and your accomplishments you
have some work to do. Your self-esteem takes the
hardest and most direct hit when life gets hard. Self-
esteem is your overall feeling of worth and personal
value. As adult women, many of us are ashamed to
admit that we still struggle with these feelings, but why
else would we continuously put ourselves in
compromising situations (promiscuity, disrespectful and
abusive relationships, etc.?)

WORDS OF ~~WISDOM~~ WINNING

"You will never gain value outside yourself."

"Close the Curtain of your Soul"

Did you know that every time you engage in questionable activities and conversations you unconsciously show the world how you feel about yourself and what you are willing to accept? This also makes you vulnerable to the "users" of the world. You know those people that are always looking to gain "something for nothing!" In my grandfather William's voice, "a crook!" Most users have mastered the art of observation and manipulation. They can smell low self-esteem a mile away and many of them are very attentive to your mental and emotional needs because they plan to use them against you. Haven't you wondered why you always attract certain types of people? The reason, believe it or not, is that many times we personify our shortcomings without realizing it.

Some of us don't know our self-esteem issues are obvious and others don't know they have them. It could be a family heirloom or maybe it's popular in your social group. Either way, your compromises seem normal because you have nothing else to compare them to. Your self-esteem might be low if you:

• Have ever sacrificed your reputation to gain attention (skimpy clothes, dirty dancing, unladylike acts, promiscuity, etc.)

• Have "shaky" boundaries (very tolerant of the

inappropriate behavior).

• Self-Sabotage (behave in ways that are not in your own best interests).

• Are immature in relationships (unreasonable expectations, always on the defense, needy etc.)

Listen, we all live, learn, and grow so don't beat yourself up if this comes as a surprise to you. Many of our social environments (inner circles, households etc.) don't give us another point of view! We don't question it because there is seemingly nothing to question. So, just mentally pick yourself up out of these places and walk in the opposite direction.

"From Rebellion to Repair"

"Don't worry about anything, but pray about everything. With thankful hearts offer up your prayers and requests to God. 7 Then, because you belong to Christ Jesus, God will bless you with peace that no one can completely understand. And this peace will control the way you think and feel." **Philippians 4:6-7**

I remember as a teenager feeling awkward and shy outside of my immediate family because, one, I didn't feel attractive and, two, I felt like I was looked down upon because of my personal issues. Picture it...skinny, acne had taken over my face, and my parents were having growing pains. Doesn't seem like much, but to a teenager with low self-esteem it felt like the end of the world. Although, I did not have a lot of control over my personal issues, I had complete control over how I handled myself so I took to prayer. Although, I only came to this conclusion after many failed attempts at rebellion. Thank God for my parents' "tight leash" because without them my insecurities would have eventually led me to do things that could have changed the course of my life.

Between my parents running interference I prayed, and I asked God some real questions about who I was and who I was supposed to be. I know by now you are thinking, "Does this woman pray about everything?" The answer is yes! I remember when my dad taught me to pray as a kid. He said, "Whatever you need, God's got it." That stuck with me and has helped me overcome my own battles with self-esteem. During this season of prayer God made me see my potential and he constantly reminded me of things that made me great. He even revealed things to me that I had not previously seen in myself. Hindsight being 20/20, as my faith in God grew so did my confidence. God didn't change my circumstances, he changed me. I became more concerned with my future and less about my physical appearance and those people that constantly discounted me. The more you get to know God you will understand that one of his greatest works in your life will be on your perspective (or point of view). Perspective is another awesome gift from God, because it means you can be standing in a thunderstorm and focused on the silhouette of the sun behind the clouds.

WORDS OF ~~WISDOM~~ WINNING

"Greatness Defined"

In history, a woman's value was only measured by her mate, but today in many ways (educationally, financially, etc.) we stand shoulder to shoulder or have surpassed our male counterparts. This presents one of the greatest illusions. Your bank account, car, and house does not make you socially equal to a man. Fair or not, even if we work like men, we still have to act like ladies if we ever intend to gain access to the things money can't buy (e.g., a God-fearing husband who is passionate about his role as your provider and protector.)

I have a theory that when our mothers and mother-figures were secretly pushing us to be more self-sufficient than they were many of us lost sight of what it truly meant to be a woman. We let the hustle take priority over husbands, give money more attention than motherhood, and a single woman's success supported her "make a man feel less than" habit. I believe success has proven to be a bittersweet victory for many of us because we view it as complete equality. However, society dictates that a woman that "lies down with dogs gets up with fleas", but a man that does the same gets up a man. I am a firm believer that a woman that does not bring anything to the table might not eat, so I am not saying that women shouldn't strive for greatness, but we have to define it. A great woman needs the will of Harriet, the ambition of Oprah, the submission of Coretta, the poise of Michelle, the spirit of Mother

Teresa, and the restraint of Mary, collectively.

13 GET READY!

"Jesus saith …. I am the way, the truth, and the life: no man cometh unto the Father, but by me."

John 14:6

Most of us claim to know God, but much of our education is second-hand. We gain this knowledge through other people (relatives, church members, preachers, etc.). Don't misunderstand me, these are great introductions, but without a personal relationship with God you can't be 100% sure the information you are getting is the most accurate execution for your life. You remember playing the gossip game when you were a kid; the last person never got the initial communication quite right. Since life is not a game you cannot risk getting mixed messages. It is vital that you get to know God for yourself. When I started my personal journey with God my initial emotion was shame. I was embarrassed by all the times I knew better and still went against God's law. However, he quickly referenced me to Adam and Eve. He knew they were naked before they disobeyed him, so disregarded those feelings of shame and embarrassment. He has been there all the time and wherever you are is a perfect place for him to prepare you to be blessed.

"Delay or Denial?"

As your relationship with God grows, you will gain a greater understanding and respect for prayer. The first thing you must realize is that your prayers are not only intended to activate God, but you as well. This is simplified in James 2:14, which poses the question,

"What good is it, my brothers, if someone says he has faith but does not have works? Can that faith save him?" Can the message be any clearer? As soon as you get off your knees you should start working toward bringing your prayers to life. If you pray to God and your answers never come, the first thing you should do is search yourself because you might be the cause of your own delay.

Analyze what you asked God for. Make sure your prayers line up with the Word of God. He will not honor your sin or prayers that request that he sin on your behalf. Also ask yourself, "Will what I asked of God harm me?" Truthfully, when our prayers are not answered deep down we know why. It's not until "knowing better" and "doing better" work together will we ever truly see our struggles' end.

Next, be very careful how you enter the presence of God. Many of our prayers go unanswered because we take baggage like envy, fear, and anger into our prayer time. Check these feelings before you go to God. It's deceitful of you to go to God about something or someone and your intentions are not pure. You remember when you prayed that your malicious co-worker is fired. She might have been wrong, but remember God is her father too. Pray that she is elevated to a better position; away from you. This way you don't wish negativity on her, and you don't have to deal with the repercussions of wishing her harm. Mathew 6:7 instructs us on how to approach prayer. It reads: "…when you pray, do not heap up empty phrases as the Gentiles do, for they think that they will be heard for their many words." If you are harboring sinful thoughts, emotions, or actions it will be difficult to be sincere with God.

Many times our delayed responses have less to do with what we ask and more to do with how we ask it. I learned from experience that there is a very distinct difference in asking God "why" and asking God for the lesson. Simply asking "why" can be very complicated because sometimes what you're dealing with could be about more than one person and for more than one reason; however, the lesson is specific just to you, for your benefit.

"The Relationship"

Sin even feels different when you get into a personal

relationship with God. Guilt (or conviction), ironically enough, will become your best friend. Before your relationship with God grew stronger consequence was your wake up call, but when you get in partnership with God you will be extremely sensitive to even the slightest misstep. This is when I first truly saw God as a parent. After this introduction God started to reveal life to me like never before.

"Blessed are the pure of heart for they shall see God." **Mathew 5: 8**

Most would think that this scripture is referring to seeing God in heaven, but my experiences have taught me that if I don't see God in this life more than likely I won't see him in the next. The question then becomes, "Where is he?" He shows his face all the time. Remember when you got that job you didn't deserve, when that stranger gave you that word of encouragement you so desperately needed, when everybody got laid-off but you, when you walked away from that totaled car, and every time you made it out of a potentially destructive situation without a scratch. God showed his face.

God's Favor"

God knows that it can be hard to follow him, especially when it's more socially acceptable not to, but he will reward your obedience with favor. He will restore the things you gave up to follow him and even give you an all-access pass to your dreams! Many people will view you as "lucky" or question how you got where you are, but favor is not fair or free! Women that find themselves in God's favor are not exempt from pain.

However, they understand that everything has purpose and this gives them a sense of comfort in tough times. God's favor is like having a backstage pass to a concert. The ticket was expensive, but now you are allowed into places you are not qualified to be in. You will be on a first name basis with very important people, and you will have opportunities that others would consider "luck!" This is what God does for those of us who have the wisdom to accept the lessons life's trials were designed to teach, the patience to be led by God, and the courage to walk with your head up in tough times.

"God's Permission"

I was born and raised in a very rural area. I am a country girl who moved to a larger city for better opportunities just three years after I finished college.

My faith in God during that season of my life was uncommon. I was fueled by the fact that I had been through a lot and survived, but most importantly I was confident in the fact that I had God's permission. Before I left home I prayed and I asked God specifically, "If it is not your will for me to move, lock every door that I knock on." As a result, I walked into every interview with the peace of the Holy Spirit because I knew I had God's blessing to at least try. Not only was I hired the day after my first interview, I was also accepted into graduate school. I knew God was with me and this was the most amazing feeling in the world.

I was 23 years old when I started my new job and because of this many of my colleagues gave me a hard time because they couldn't understand how someone so young could speak with such authority. God eventually promoted me to a supervisory role and those same colleagues were furious. The looks on their faces said, "Who does she think she is?" It was inappropriate to respond, but in my mind I thought, A King's kid, that's who! When I finished my graduate program I understood the difficulty many people were having moving into leadership roles. The market was flooded. In other words, a lot of people had the same degrees, but very few jobs were available. One of my colleagues said it had been 15 years since he received his degree and he still did not have a position. I responded before I knew it. "You better get to know God!" When you get God's permission, you can speak with confidence to his promises. I received my Master's degree in May 2006 and was in a leadership role by May 2007.

14 GET SET!

"If we say that we have no sin, we deceive ourselves, and the truth is not in us."

1 John 1:8

We have all, at some point in life, pondered why the next woman seems to live better than we do. She seems happy, full of life, focused, and fabulous! When she was younger she did what everybody else did, but little by little she began to separate herself from the behavior. She is still far from perfect, but has the audacity to participate in praise and worship. Many of you would say this woman is "playing with God," but I have some ground breaking news for you. God has infinite intelligence and you can't possibly be smart enough to play him.

On the contrary, missing God's will for your life, because the status quo is to avoid engaging in any type of worship because of your sins, is suicide to your well-being and you, my dear, are the one being played. If the only people that could serve God were those without sin there would be no place in society for a church. We are all imperfect. If you wait until you "get yourself together" to go to God you will never get the opportunity. Furthermore, if you had the ability to get it together you would have kept it together in the first place. So stop being a prisoner to public opinion and be led by your own spirit.

You have to own your mess and your best! This is the only way you can stand level with your future.

Repeat after me,

"I will no longer be held captive by **(fill in the foundational reason for your current state of struggle)**. Although I have been wounded, I survived and from this day forward I will live as a conqueror." A conqueror is one who overcomes by mental, physical, and moral force. Each of these forces must become active in your life if you expect to reach your destiny. The mental process starts every morning with the previous quotation, repeat it as many times as necessary during the day to stay focused. Next, you have to deny yourself the physical activities that placed you in the negative state of being or those that you picked up in your attempt to cope. When you master the mental, the physical becomes easier; the two operate like a math problem, one builds on the other.

When you arrive at the place where you have empathy for people in situations similar to those that you have overcome you have found morality. This marks the end of paralyzing pain and the beginning of infinite possibility. When negativity is all around you it is human nature to start second-guessing your worth as a woman. However, it is **unnatural** to allow this negativity to lead you to devalue and degrade yourself. You are a big girl now! You know that pain has divine purpose and no matter how much it hurts physically, your spiritual strength is much more powerful. When bad things happen brace yourself; the weight of the experience will make you stronger. Look for the built-in blessing, and understand that things you are going through are merely the "labor pains" for purpose.

"Untie God's Hands"

"You will not need to fight in this battle. Stand firm, hold your position, and see the salvation of the Lord on your behalf.........................."

2 Chronicle 20:17

Emotional healing is a very spiritual journey and when you get to the place were change is mandatory this scripture will become its clearest. This encouragement from God was spoken through Jahaziel before a battle. However, I want you to let it speak to the battles in your life. God is saying "Be strong, stand on my Word, and let me handle it! I know you are tired, but I can only make it alright if you listen to my instructions and let me be God." God does not want to see you in pain, but it is only until you allow his will for life to become more important than your own; will you see God's best become active in your life.

"The Spirit of Fear"

I was afraid of God's will for a long time. I would find myself praying and not being able to say "Lord let your will be done." The words scared me because I had plans. I was extremely ambitious and this was fueled less by my determination to succeed and more by my determination never to go back to feeling "less than" again. When I was in college, I prayed that God bless the work of my hands. I specifically said, "Let everything I touch, as long as it's positive and productive, turn to gold."

Platinum wasn't popular yet. God honored me. I worked hard and so did he on my behalf. Unfortunately, I became a control freak and very self-righteous. God took the next four years of my life to show me that I was in control of nothing. Those were four of the hardest years I ever experienced, but they also blessed me in a way that I cannot describe. I know you are wondering how it could be both. It is just the wonder of God. I was newly married and just started miscarrying babies left and right. Many tests were ran to try to find the cause; but doctors deemed me healthy. So I asked God, "If I am healthy what are you trying to teach me?"

WORDS OF WINNING ~~WISDOM~~

Questions are the keys to understanding God's plan for your life.

Day and night I prayed this prayer and not only did I learn my purpose, but I also learned that God's will for my life was much more rewarding than anything I had ever "planned." The education I received during this time of my life I could have never gotten if I was happy. Happy people have a tendency to be hasty with God. We pray, but we are not as attentive as we are when we are desperate and in need. When I finally had my son the pregnancy was flawless, not one complication.

WINNING
WORDS OF ~~WISDOM~~

If you find yourself in a season of life where nothing makes sense, <u>God's</u> class might be in session.

The Benediction

I laughed when I finished writing because it was not my initial intention to write a book so drenched with scripture and commentary about God, but you got me! I would have given up years ago if I had not taken special interest in God and more importantly he in me. I know how it feels to be broken by life, but I also know how it feels to be happy, blessed, favored, and at peace. To say the least, God made good on his promise to me and he wants to do the same for you, but you have to snap out of the "Woe is me" mindset. It is perfectly natural to become upset and even cry when faced with the trials of life. Jesus wept (John 11:35). However, you should not be led by these emotions, and this can be accomplished by simply taking a deep breath and praying for strength, direction, and self-control or by taping your mouth shut and your feet together. Only you know what works for you.

Take a trip down memory lane and go back to the day before tragedy struck. What were your goals? What did you want out of life? This is where you start. If you feel as though you have never seen "better days," be confident in the fact that God will eventually level the playing field and you will be able to choose your path to greatness.

You should not only expect better, you should work towards it, and when opportunity presents itself, walk confidently into it. We are all carrying something negative, but my hope is that you are carrying it in your pocket and not on your back. Let it serve as a small reminder of how strong you are and not the greatest

hindrance of your life.

Psalms 37:1-5, states, "…Trust in the Lord and do

good. Then you will live safely in the land and prosper.

Take delight in the Lord, and he will give you your

heart's desires. Commit everything you do to the Lord.

Trust him, and he will help you."

We are all God's children and as a parent he has given

us everything we need to reach our fullest potential.

Those goals you had as a little girl weren't random. God

was giving you a choice. He planted those dreams in

your heart and mind because he knew that they would

be perfect for your skill set. It was in those dreams that

your quality of life would be at its greatest, but life

happened and you lost focus. Your choice to pacify

your pain with negativity led you off the path to greatness. The time has come for you to go back and pick up where you fell off because those same blessings that were assigned to you before "life happened" are still yours. God's power and your obedience will give you the opportunity to take your life back and allow you live out your dreams.

Let's Pray

"God, it is in the name of Jesus that I ask you to cleanse our hearts and minds of the negativity that drove faith out of our lives. Lord, make our greatness clear and make us fearless as we fight for what is ours. Lord, finally, I ask that you give us the strength to use our gifts to better our lives and the lives of those around us.

Forgive us for doubting you. We thank you in advance for this. Amen."

If you have not already figured it out, struggle is not your enemy, but when the time comes it will serve as a clear demonstration of how strong you are. Look back over your life at the mountains you were able to climb. Those mountains gave you everything you need to live your "best life" right now! You got this! Now get back in the race and always remember tough times don't last tough women do. **Ready, Set, Grow.**

NOTES

NOTES

NOTES